W9-BVM-724

Platypus
A Century-long Mystery

by William Caper

Consultant: Dr. Melody Serena
Conservation Biologist with the Australian Platypus Conservancy

BEARPORT
PUBLISHING

New York, New York

2980465
DISCARDED
Alexander Mitchell Library
Aberdeen, SD 57401

Credits

Cover and Title Page, © Dave Watts/Bios/Peter Arnold Inc.; TOC, © Shin Yoshino/Minden Pictures; 4-5, © Dave Watts/NHPA/Photoshot; 7, © Martin Rugner/Superstock; 7TR, © Wrennie/ iStockphoto; 7BL, © Robyn Butler/Shutterstock; 8, © Kevin Fleming/Corbis; 9, © D. Parer & E. Parer-Cook/Auscape/Minden Pictures; 10, © Andrew McCutcheon; 11T, © blickwinkel/Lenz/ Alamy; 11B, © Jupiterimages/Stock Image/Alamy; 12, © Dave Watts/Alamy; 13, © David Doubilet; 14, © National Library of Australia; 15, © National Library of Australia; 16, © David Doubilet; 17, © B. G. Thomson/Photo Researchers, Inc.; 18, © Dorling Kindersley; 19, © Jason Edwards/National Geographic/Getty Images; 20T, © Jason Edwards/National Geographic; 20B, © Gunther Schmida/ Lochman Transparencies; 21, © Jason Edwards/National Geographic/Getty Images; 21BL, © Theo Allofs/Corbis; 21TR, © Dave Watts/Bios/Peter Arnold Inc.; 22, © Dave Watts/NHPA/Photoshot; 23T, © David Doubilet; 23B, © David Doubilet; 24, © David Doubilet/National Geographic; 25, © Alicia Carter/www.wiresnr.org; 26, © David Doubilet; 27, © Geoff Williams/Australian Platypus Conservancy; 28, © Nicole Duplaix/National Geographic/Getty Images; 29T, © ANT Photo Library/Photo Researchers, Inc.; 29B, © Thorsten Milse/Robert Harding Picture Library Ltd/Alamy; 31, © D. Parer & E. Parer-Cook/Auscape/Minden Pictures.

Publisher: Kenn Goin
Editorial Director: Adam Siegel
Creative Director: Spencer Brinker
Design: Dawn Beard Creative
Photo Researcher: Beaura Kathy Ringrose

Library of Congress Cataloging-in-Publication Data

Caper, William.
  Platypus : a century-long mystery / by William Caper.
      p. cm. — (Uncommon animals)
  Includes bibliographical references and index.
  ISBN-13: 978-1-59716-735-2 (library binding)
  ISBN-10: 1-59716-735-5 (library binding)
  1. Platypus—Juvenile literature. I. Title.

  QL737.M72C37 2009
  599.2'9—dc22

                              2008013543

Copyright © 2009 Bearport Publishing Company, Inc. All rights reserved. No part of this publication may be reproduced in whole or in part, stored in a retrieval system, or transmitted in any form or by any means, electronic, mechanical, photocopying, recording, or otherwise, without written permission from the publisher.

For more information, write to Bearport Publishing Company, Inc., 101 Fifth Avenue, Suite 6R, New York, New York 10003. Printed in the United States of America.

10 9 8 7 6 5 4 3 2 1

Contents

What in the World Is It?

One day in 1798, John Hunter, the Governor of Australia, went for a walk. He saw an **Aborigine** hunting near a river. The man was using a spear to kill an animal in the water.

Aborigines were the first people to live in Australia. They have lived there for more than 40,000 years.

When Hunter looked at the dead creature, he was shocked. He had never seen such an odd-looking animal before. It had a **bill** like a duck and a tail like a beaver. He wanted to learn more about this bizarre creature. So Hunter packed the animal's skin in a barrel and sent it to scientists in England. Perhaps they could figure out what it was.

John Hunter was amazed to see an animal that looked like this one. It had a bill, fur, webbed feet, claws, and a wide tail.

Send More Bizarre Creatures!

What kind of strange animal had the Governor of Australia sent to England? Scientists were eager to begin solving this mystery. However, they needed more of the creatures from Australia to study.

Platypuses in the Wild

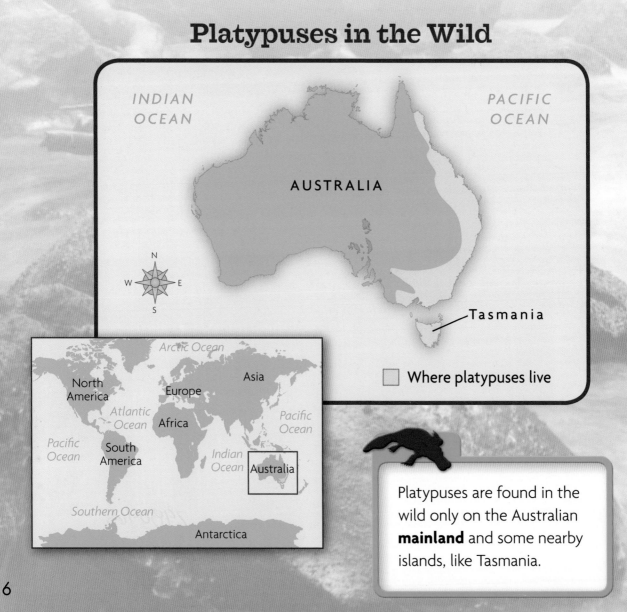

INDIAN OCEAN

PACIFIC OCEAN

AUSTRALIA

Tasmania

N W E S

☐ Where platypuses live

Arctic Ocean

North America

Europe

Asia

Atlantic Ocean

Africa

Pacific Ocean

Pacific Ocean

South America

Indian Ocean

Australia

Southern Ocean

Antarctica

Platypuses are found in the wild only on the Australian **mainland** and some nearby islands, like Tasmania.

Unfortunately, it wasn't easy to capture the shy animals. They disappeared under the water if anyone came too close. The only way to catch them was to shoot them from far away. English scientists would have to learn about the animal by studying dead ones.

koala

Animals besides the platypus that are found only in Australia include the kangaroo, koala, and wombat.

kangaroo

wombat

Is It Real?

The first question English scientists wanted to answer was: Is this animal real? In Asia, **taxidermists** sometimes sewed together parts of different dead animals. They might sew the head of a monkey to the body of a fish. These fake animals were sold as **souvenirs**.

This fake creature was made by combining body parts from different animals.

Was this unusual creature from Australia a fake? Had someone sewn a duck's bill to the body of a beaver or a **mole**? Scientists couldn't find any signs that the body parts had been sewn together. So they finally agreed that the animal was real. They also gave it a name. In 1799, scientist George Shaw named the strange-looking creature the platypus.

Platypus comes from two Greek words—*platus*, meaning "flat," and *pous*, meaning "foot." Platypus was a good name for an animal with flat, webbed feet.

Bird, Reptile, or Mammal?

The platypus had a name. Yet scientists still did not know what kind of animal it was. Platypuses look and act like many different kinds of creatures. Their bills look like the bills of some birds, such as ducks. They spend a lot of time in the water like some **reptiles**, such as crocodiles. They are also furry like **mammals**.

According to an Aborigine **legend**, the first platypus was the **offspring** of a duck and a water rat.

A water rat in the wild

Was the platypus a kind of bird, reptile, or mammal? To figure that out, scientists needed to learn how platypuses **reproduce** and raise their young. Female mammals give birth to live young and feed them with their milk. Birds and most reptiles lay eggs, but do not provide milk for their young. What did the platypus do?

All baby mammals, such as puppies, drink milk from their mother's body.

All birds and most reptiles, such as crocodiles, hatch from eggs.

A Very Shy Animal

Someone would have to catch a live platypus or study them in the wild to find out whether they laid eggs or gave birth to live young. It isn't easy to **observe** platypuses in their natural **habitat**, however.

The animals sleep during the day in **burrows** near rivers or lakes. Entrances to these underground homes are hidden by plants or located below the surface of the water.

This platypus is leaving its burrow. A platypus burrow can be 1 foot (.3 m) or deeper underground. The tunnel leading to the burrow can be up to 100 feet (30 m) long.

When platypuses are awake, they hunt for food in the water. Yet they hunt mainly at night, when they're harder to spot. They are also easily frightened. Since finding and studying platypuses in the wild is hard, it was difficult for scientists to learn how the animals reproduce.

Platypuses rarely come onto dry land, so they leave few footprints. This makes them hard to track and study.

Some Luck . . . But Not Enough

Finally, in 1832, a **naturalist** named George Bennett caught several live platypuses in eastern Australia. Bennett had help from local Aborigines who were familiar with the area. They helped Bennett find and dig up platypus burrows. He was able to catch one male and two females.

Aborigines were skilled hunters who knew how to find many animals in the wild, including kangaroos and platypuses.

Bennett's success didn't last long, though. Platypuses aren't able to live easily in **captivity** unless they are cared for properly. One female died just by being bumped around in its box on the horse ride to Bennett's home. Another died soon after because Bennett didn't know what to feed it. If platypuses couldn't live in captivity, would the mystery of how they reproduce and raise their young ever be solved?

For more than fifty years, George Bennett tried to find out how platypuses reproduce.

Solving the Mystery

As it turned out, scientists solved the egg mystery without a live platypus. In 1884, scientist William Caldwell shot a female platypus by the Burnett River in eastern Australia. She had just laid an egg. Caldwell also found a second egg in her body that was about to be laid.

Platypus eggs are much smaller than chicken eggs.

Scientists now knew that female platypuses lay eggs, like birds or reptiles. Years earlier, however, scientists had learned that female platypuses make milk for their young, like mammals. So it turned out that the platypus behaved like different kinds of animals. As a result, scientists decided to put the platypus in a special **category** in the mammal group, called monotremes (MAH-nuh-treemz). These mammals lay eggs instead of having live young.

Only one other kind of mammal—echidnas (ih-KID-nuhz)—lay eggs. Scientists also placed this rare mammal in the monotremes group.

The echidna, or spiny anteater, also lives in Australia.

From Eggs to Babies

After almost 100 years, the mystery of how platypuses have young was solved. Yet other questions remained. For example, how did platypuses care for their eggs and babies?

Over time, scientists learned that a female platypus in the wild lays one to three eggs at a time in her burrow. She places the eggs between her belly and tail to keep them warm.

This illustration shows how a mother platypus uses her belly to keeps her eggs warm.

After they **hatch**, the babies are about the size of kidney beans. Their mother's milk makes them strong. The babies are able to leave the burrow for the first time at four months. About two months later, they are ready to go off on their own.

Baby platypuses

Baby platypuses don't have any fur and can't see when they are born. By the time they are 14 weeks old their bodies are covered with fur and they can see.

Platypus Prey

In the 1940s, scientist David Fleay became the first person to **breed** platypuses in captivity. He was able to keep the platypuses alive because scientists had learned what these animals need to eat.

Platypus **prey** includes small shellfish, crayfish, freshwater shrimp, insects, and worms. They need to eat a lot of these animals, too. A platypus can eat up to one-third its body weight each day.

Platypuses have no teeth. Instead of chewing food, they grind it up using hard pads in their bills.

Platypuses eat small animals, such as freshwater shrimp.

To find prey, a platypus dives to the bottom of a lake or river. It can hold its breath for up to three minutes when swimming underwater. After it locates food, the platypus uses its bill to scoop it up. Then it swims to the surface to eat.

Many kinds of animals hunt platypuses for food. These **predators** include crocodiles, dingoes (wild dogs), and foxes.

fox

dingo

crocodile

Learning More All the Time

As late as the 1980s, scientists were still finding out more about how platypuses find food. When a platypus dives, it closes its eyes in order to keep water out. So how does it find prey?

All moving animals give off electrical signals. A platypus's sensitive bill can pick up these signals. This way of finding food is called **electrolocation**.

A platypus hunting for food

Even today, scientists are working to learn more about the platypus. The male platypus has sharp, fang-like spurs on both of its rear ankles. These spurs release **venom**, which can cause great pain to humans. It's even strong enough to kill a dog. Scientists haven't found a cure for the poison yet, but they are still trying.

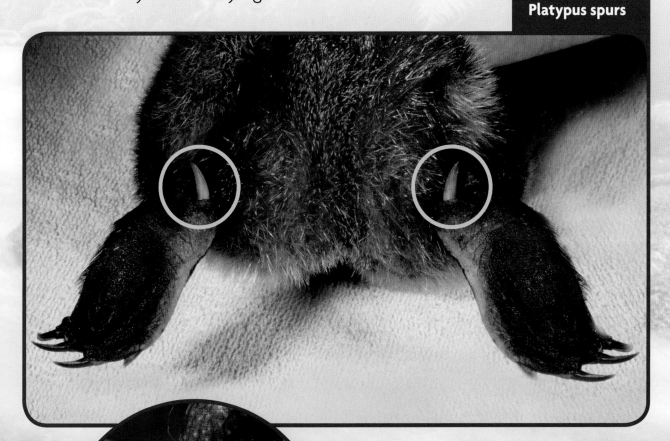

Platypus spurs

Male platypuses usually use their spurs to fight other males for a **mate**. Sometimes, they use the spurs to defend themselves against predators.

Tracking the Platypus Today

Today, researchers are still trying to catch and study the shy animal. **Biologist** Melody Serena studies wild platypuses in Australia. She safely traps them using special nets. After catching an animal, Melody weighs and measures it. She implants a **microchip** in the platypus so it can be identified if it is caught again. Then she releases the animal back into the water.

Melody Serena with a captured platypus

Unfortunately, there are now fewer platypuses to study than ever before. Trash that people throw near rivers and lakes can be deadly. Platypuses can cut themselves on broken glass or tin cans. In addition, some of the animals get caught in fishing nets and drown.

The group Wildlife Information, Rescue and Education Service (WIRES) cares for injured or sick animals, like this platypus. They then release them back into the wild.

People used to hunt platypuses so that they could use their fur to make coats and caps. Since the 1920s, however, it has been against the law to kill platypuses.

Still a Puzzle

Despite the dangers to platypuses, Melody is hopeful. Scientists once thought that the shy animals could only live in areas that were far away from people. Recently, however, Melody has found many platypuses living in the waterways of Australia's second-largest city—Melbourne. Melody says that finding platypuses "living near busy roads and factories has been a very exciting discovery."

Platypuses live in rivers near Melbourne, including the Yarra River, in eastern Australia.

The best times for Australians to spot a wild platypus is at dusk or dawn.

Mysteries still remain about this uncommon animal. For example, because platypuses are so shy, researchers don't know how many there are in the wild. Luckily, these animals are not thought to be in danger of **extinction**. The mysterious platypus is a survivor that continues to surprise and amaze people.

In 18 years, Melody Serena has been able to trap and release nearly 1,000 platypuses.

Platypus Facts

The platypus is a very unusual-looking mammal. It has a **flexible** bill, a wide tail, and webbed feet with claws. The platypus is one of only two kinds of mammals that lay eggs to reproduce. Here are some other facts about this uncommon animal.

Weight	**males:** 2.6–5.7 pounds (1.2–2.6 kg) **females:** 1.5–3.5 pounds (.7–1.6 kg)
Length	**males:** usually about 20 inches (51 cm) long **females:** usually about 17 inches (43 cm) long
Food	small shellfish, crayfish, freshwater shrimp, insects, worms, and fish eggs
Life Span	may live up to 21 years in the wild
Habitat	in and along the rivers, creeks, and lakes of eastern Australia and nearby islands, such as Tasmania
Population	unknown

More Uncommon Animals

The platypus is one kind of uncommon animal in Australia. Many other unusual animals also live there.

Short-beaked Echidna

- The short-beaked echidna's favorite foods are ants and termites. It is often called the "spiny anteater."
- When frightened, the echidna curls up into a tight ball with its sharp spines pointing out.
- The echidna has no teeth. It grinds its food between its tongue and the bottom of its mouth.
- Like the male platypus, the male echidna has spurs on its back legs. However, the echidna's spurs do not contain venom.

Wombat

- Wombats are small bear-like animals that are found only in Australia and nearby islands, such as Tasmania.
- Wombats use their claws to dig burrows. They stay in their burrows during the day and come out at night to look for food.
- Wombats have sharp front teeth that never stop growing.
- The wombat's favorite food is grass. It will also feed on roots and bark.
- A mother wombat has a special pouch on her belly where her baby grows and develops. The baby wombat stays in its mother's pouch for about seven months.

Glossary

Aborigine (*ab*-uh-RIJ-uh-nee) a native person of Australia

bill (BILL) the part of a platypus's mouth that looks like the beak of some birds

biologist (bye-OL-uh-jist) a scientist who studies plants and animals

breed (BREED) to produce young

burrows (BUR-ohz) tunnels or holes in the ground made by some animals for shelter

captivity (kap-TIV-uh-tee) places where animals live in which they are cared for by people, and which are not the animals' natural homes

category (KAT-uh-*gor*-ee) a group of similar things

electrolocation (i-*lek*-troh-loh-KAY-shuhn) finding things by sensing electrical signals

extinction (ek-STINGK-shuhn) when a type of animal or plant dies out; there are no more alive on Earth

flexible (FLEK-suh-buhl) able to bend

habitat (HAB-uh-*tat*) the place in nature where a plant or animal normally lives

hatch (HACH) to come out of an egg

legend (LEJ-uhnd) a story from the past that is often not entirely true

mainland (MAYN-luhnd) the largest land mass of a country

mammals (MAM-uhlz) warm-blooded animals that have a backbone, hair or fur on their skin, and drink their mothers' milk when they are babies

mate (MAYT) one of a pair of animals that breed together

microchip (MYE-kroh-chip) a tiny electronic device used to store information

mole (MOHL) a small furry mammal that lives mostly underground

naturalist (NACH-ur-uh-list) a person who studies plants and animals

observe (uhb-ZURV) to watch something carefully in order to learn about it

offspring (OF-spring) an animal's young

predators (PRED-uh-turz) animals that hunt other animals for food

prey (PRAY) an animal hunted by another animal for food

reproduce (ree-pruh-DOOSS) to have young

reptiles (REP-tilez) cold-blooded animals, such as lizards, snakes, turtles, or crocodiles, that have dry, scaly skin, a backbone, and lungs for breathing

souvenirs (*soo*-vuh-NIHRZ) objects that are reminders of people or places

taxidermists (TAK-suh-*dur*-mists) people who prepare, stuff, and mount dead animals

venom (VEN-uhm) poison made by some animals

Bibliography

Moyal, Ann. *Platypus: The Extraordinary Story of How a Curious Creature Baffled the World.* Baltimore, MD: The Johns Hopkins University Press (2004).

Serena, Melody. "Duck-billed Platypus: Australia's Urban Oddity," *National Geographic* Vol. 197, No. 4 (April 2000), 118–129.

animals.nationalgeographic.com/animals/mammals/platypus.html?nav=A-Z

www.bbc.co.uk/nature/wildfacts/factfiles/681.shtml

www.platypus.asn.au

Read More

Brice, Jo. *The Platypus: What Is It?* Ringwood, Victoria, New South Wales: Puffin Books (2000).

Collard III, Sneed B. *A Platypus, Probably.* Watertown, MA: Charlesbridge Publishing (2005).

Myers, Jack. *The Puzzle of the Platypus: And Other Explorations of Science in Action.* Honesdale, PA: Boyds Mills Press (2008).

Short, Joan, Jack Green, and Bettina Bird. *Platypus.* New York: Mondo Publishing (1997).

Learn More Online

To learn more about platypuses, visit
www.bearportpublishing.com/UncommonAnimals

Index

About the Author

William Caper has written books about history, science, film, and many other topics. He lives in San Francisco with his wife, Erin, and their dog, Face.